THE
*Archive Photographs*
SERIES

# BRISTOL AEROPLANE
## COMPANY

By the same author
*Gloster Aircraft Company*

THE
*Archive Photographs*
SERIES

# BRISTOL AEROPLANE COMPANY

Published to mark the 85th Anniversary
of the founding of
the British and Colonial Aeroplane Company

*Compiled by*
Derek N. James IEng, AMRAeS

*For all former employees of the*
*Bristol Aeroplane Company*

CHALFORD

First published 1996
Copyright © Derek N. James, 1996

The Chalford Publishing Company
St Mary's Mill, Chalford,
Stroud, Gloucestershire, GL6 8NX

ISBN 0 7524 0362 1

Typesetting and origination by
The Chalford Publishing Company
Printed in Great Britain by
Redwood Books, Trowbridge

Other titles in
THE *Archive Photographs Aviation* SERIES

*Gloster Aircraft Company*
*Shorts Aircraft*
*Filton and the Flying Machine*

in preparation

*Boulton Paul*
*De Havilland*
*Farnborough Air Shows*
*Hawker*
*Supermarine*
*Vickers*

# Contents

Experience creates excellence. Bristol had built some 12,430 aeroplanes before producing these two Britannia airliners. The first pair of thirty-three delivered to British Overseas Airways Corporation, they are seen in January 1956 at London Heathrow Airport. Note the airline's Speedbird motif on the building.

# Company History

I make no apology for virtually repeating here the opening sentence of my *Gloster Aircraft Company* book in this series. It is just as relevant to the history of the great Bristol Aeroplane Company. For those who have not yet read 'Gloster', here is that sentence: 'The names of Britain's pioneering aircraft designers and pilots who founded their own companies are well known. Among them are Sopwith, Handley Page, Fairey and Blackburn.' Now read on, please.

All these men were engineers. They had no great knowledge of big business organization and most were always short of cash to keep their infant enterprises afloat – or should that be 'airborne'?

Then there was wealthy George White. He was something else. When he entered the aviation business he was already Sir George White, Bt. He was described as 'a dapper little Edwardian, fierce in manner, with tireless energy and a "take-over outlook" in business affairs.' Aged 20, and with a legal background, he became secretary of the small company formed to start an electric tramways system in Bristol. Later he provided Bristol with its first motor omnibus services and taxicabs. Soon he left the legal profession, entered the Bristol Stock Exchange, and began investing in transport businesses in Gloucester, Bath, and many other parts of England. He was to become chief of the Bristol Tramways Co. and Stock Exchange president.

During a 1909 visit to the south of France for health reasons, Sir George attended an early flying meeting in Pau, where he saw Louis Paulhan flying a Voisin aeroplane. He was immediately captivated by the possibilities of this new form of transport. Hearing that Gabriel Voisin had designed one for the Société Zodiac in Paris, he at once negotiated with characteristic zeal a licence to build the Zodiac aeroplane and told his brother Samuel 'We must start an aircraft company'!

At the February 1910 Annual General Meeting of the Bristol Tramways Co., he startled shareholders by announcing his intention to do just that. He allayed their fears by stating that he, his son Stanley and his brother Samuel would shoulder the risks and the cost of establishing such a company. Cannily, he told them that it would lease their company's omnibus depot at Filton, four miles from the city. This would attract people onto trams travelling to Filton to see the flying demonstrations he planned to organise there.

When Sir George established the British and Colonial Aeroplane Company (BCAC) in February 1910, unlike those infant companies of most other pioneers, it began operation with £25,000 capital subscribed by himself, his brother Samuel and his son G. Stanley White. His nephews Henry White-Smith and Sydney Smith also provided finance, while their brother,

William Verdon-Smith, and his wife's nephew Herbert Thomas were founding directors too. Truly this was a Bristol family-run business.

An interesting sidelight on the company name came to light during research for this book. A 1911 photograph of the company's hangar at Larkhill shows the name as 'The Bristol and Colonial Aeroplane Co Ltd'. Sir George actually registered four slightly different company names but chose to use the one in the above paragraph. The Larkhill name, however, was not one of the other three!

In addition to building Zodiac biplanes at Filton, Sir George ordered a French-built example which was supplied with a guarantee to fly! Unfortunately, this machine refused to get off the ground. Maurice Edmond, the reputable French pilot engaged to fly it, recommended that 'it be pushed into a corner and forgotten'. Sir George agreed, stopped Zodiac production and wrote off this exercise to experience. However, he wrested 15,000 francs compensation from the Zodiac company for not supplying an aeroplane which could fly.

In order to get restarted, George Challenger, BCAC's chief engineer, on Sir George's instructions, studied the biplane designs of Henri Farman which had appeared in several aeronautical magazines. The upshot was that he produced designs for a similar aeroplane. Within three weeks it had been built, named Boxkite, and flown at Larkhill on 29th July 1910. Its pilot, Maurice Edmond, reported the handling was perfect. Sir George immediately put twenty Boxkites into production.

Believing that customers would want flying lessons, he set up schools at Brooklands and at Larkhill, Wilts, the latter attracting pupils from among Army officers stationed nearby. This interest in aviation by the 'soldiery' was not immediately well received by the War Office. It was public pressure which persuaded Capt Bertram Dickson to fly a Boxkite in the 1910 Army Manoeuvres. Scouting for the 'Red Army' in the chill misty dawn of 21 September, he spotted the advancing 'Blue Army' near Salisbury. He flew back, half frozen, and reported to Command HQ. The 'Red' top brass were ecstatic and changed their battle plan.

Dickson took off again, this time landing near a house to telephone his report to base. But he forgot he was in 'enemy' territory. Up galloped Corporal Arthur Edwards of the 'Blue' North Somerset Light Yeomanry (later apprentice supervisor with the Bristol aero-engine department) and captured Dickson, putting him 'out of action'. Despite initial War Office lack of interest, things changed: eighty per cent of British pilots available for service when war came in 1914 were BCAC-trained.

The Boxkite was soon being surpassed by faster monoplane designs. Sir George was quick to respond. While biplanes continued to be built he invited British, French and Romanian engineers to Filton to design monoplanes. But things changed with the outbreak of World War One in August 1914, when Frank Barnwell designed the Scout military single-seat biplane of which 367 were built, many serving with the Royal Flying Corps (RFC).

With only two short breaks, Barnwell produced a steady stream of designs between 1915 and 1938. Many were built as one-offs, others in quantity. They began with a couple of military two-seaters, and then came the renowned Bristol Fighter – or 'Brisfit'. It was the RFC's best two-seat fighter. A total of 5,308 were built by BCAC at Filton and Brislington and by eleven other manufacturers in the UK and USA.

A long shadow was cast over the company when Sir George White died late in the evening of 22 November 1916 aged 62. A workaholic and heavy smoker, he had been in failing health. Typically, he died as he had lived, working hard at his desk.

The first BCAC military monoplane was the M.1. BCAC built 130 of these which were flown by a handful of RFC squadrons in the Middle East. Next came the MR.7, almost, but not quite, a metal Bristol Fighter. Two were made. A closer Brisfit copy was the three-seat civil Tourer with a production run of thirty-three. Four Scouts and assorted F.2C and Badger two-seaters were followed in 1918 by a small group of four-engined triplanes, two Braemar bombers, the 14-seat Pullman and two Tramps, this latter pair never getting off the ground.

When peace broke out in November 1918 the company's 'swingometer' moved firmly towards civil aircraft. The Royal Mail Steam Packet Company's interest in flying-boat delivery of mail to South America offered hope for new work. Unfortunately, that company's preference for steam turbine-powered aircraft proved an insuperable problem for BCAC designers and work was abandoned. But other designs soon appeared.

First was the single-seat Babe in both monoplane and biplane configuration; then the Bullet, a flying engine test-bed and racer. This was followed in 1920 by the two-seat Seely; then a ten-seater, uninspiringly named the Ten-Seater, and the Brandon.

The Bullet was an integral part of a major event in BCAC history, its function being to test the Jupiter air-cooled radial engine made by Cosmos Engineering Co. of Fishponds, Bristol. In February 1920 Cosmos went into liquidation when its parent group crashed after a disastrous commercial gamble involving household goods shipped to Russia which were immediately seized by the Bolsheviks! However, Cosmos's chief engineer, Roy (later Sir Roy) Fedden, kept the design team together and working on Jupiter engines until a new owner could be found.

Meanwhile, on 23 March, the BCAC itself went into liquidation, but for a different reason. Someone discovered that by closing down BCAC and transferring its fixed assets to a new trading company – the Bristol Aeroplane Co. (BACo), one of the four registered by Sir George in 1910 – much less Excess Profits Tax would have to be paid. Thus, BACo acquired all BCAC's assets at a cost of about £300. Clearly, Sir George White's management team had his eagle-eye for the small print. But back to Cosmos Engineering.

Although Fedden's designs impressed the BACo directors, it was only with heavy Government pressure that they agreed to take over Cosmos as the nucleus of a new BACo aero-engine department at Filton. For £15,000 they got Fedden, thirty-one engineers and five Jupiter engines with a promised order for ten more – plus a load of tools, drawings and spares. Sir George would have approved.

Barnwell's Jupiter-powered Bullfinch was an all-metal single-seat fighter monoplane, convertible into a two-seat reconnaissance biplane. Two for the price of one. But it wasn't ordered. Then the Taxiplane and Primary Trainer Machines were conceived. Both used the Bristol, née Cosmos, small three-cylinder Lucifer engine. A total of twenty-eight of these two aircraft were built, some being exported. Other Bristol-powered types were the 1922 Racer, with its Jupiter totally encased in its rotund fuselage; the Bloodhound two-seater, and the Jupiter Fighters and Advanced Trainer. Altogether a bunch of twenty-six aircraft which, photographically, all looked rather bewildered.

In 1925 the Berkeley two-seat bomber temporarily broke the mould by having a Rolls-Royce Condor engine. It failed to win orders. Happily, the aero-engine department didn't depend on Bristol aeroplanes to get its products airborne. Jupiters were in worldwide service and being licence-built in France. During the harder times BACo kept the wolf from the hangar doors by making 'bus and coach bodies for Bristol Tramways Co.

Soon, the rattle of high tensile steel strip being rolled into various sections for airframe construction was being matched by the roar of 'home grown' engines. The Brownie, Boarhound, Beaver and Bagshot, the Bulldog and Bullpup (oh-the alliteration!), plus Bristol Types 109, 110A, 118 and 120 all had metal airframes and Bristol engines. Only the Badminton racer and the Type 101 two-seat fighter were of mainly wooden construction. All were biplanes, except the little Brownie and the Bagshot twin-engined fighter.

The company's last biplane, the Type 123 fighter, had cantilever (unbraced) wings and a Rolls-Royce steam-cooled Goshawk engine. This combination, like the lot of the policemen in Gilbert and Sullivan's opera The Pirates of Penzance, was 'not a happy one'. Few of these all-metal aeroplanes got beyond the prototype stage. The exception was the Bulldog. Nearly 450 were built and flown by ten RAF squadrons and eight other air forces.

When orders dried up, BACo 'took in other people's washing'. Between 1912 and 1917 it built some 1,200 BE.2s designed by the Royal Aircraft Factory at Farnborough. In 1919-20, 168 Parnall Panthers were built at Filton, followed during 1927-28 by eighty-nine Armstrong Whitworth Siskins. They were nice little earners for BACo.

Then, in May 1935, the Government finally bit the bullet, forsaking its policies of disarmament and appeasement and deciding to strengthen and modernize the RAF. It was not a moment too soon. On 15 June 1935 BACo became a public limited liability company with a 4,200 workforce – mostly in the engine factory – and a 13 acre plant. Happily, Sir Stanley White, the founder's son, was still at the helm. He had carried on the tradition of a family business since 1910.

Almost unwittingly, Bristol Aeroplane Co. was already preparing for war – with a fast twin-engined civil transport! Named *Britain First*, it was built in 1935 for Lord Rothermere, the *Daily Mail*'s owner, and was 50 m.p.h. faster than the RAF's latest biplane fighters. It was the basis for the Blenheim bomber, more than 5,500 of which were built. They flew with the RAF, and with the Air Arms of Canada, Finland, Romania and Turkey. A Blenheim was the first RAF aircraft to fly over enemy territory on 3 September 1939, the first day of World War Two.

But before that the company's workforce and facilities were greatly expanded. When war came, BACo was the world's largest single aircraft manufacturer with 2,700,000 sq ft of buildings. Bristol designs were also sub-contracted. Short and Harland built fifty Bombay bomber/transports while A.V. Roe and Rootes Securities each produced 250 Blenheims. In October 1938 a new twin-engined torpedo-bomber, named Beaufort with the Duke of Beaufort's permission, appeared in Bristol skies. In total 1,429 were built at Filton and Banwell and another 700 in Australia.

The death of Frank Barnwell on 2 August 1938 in the crash of his own-design light aeroplane robbed BACo and the aircraft industry of one of its most innovative and prolific designers. With Barnwell's death, Leslie Frise, who had shared much of the design work with him since the Bulldog days, became responsible for design for the next decade.

The RAF's lack of a long-range cannon-armed fighter was met, in 1939, by the Beaufighter. A heavily-armed aircraft able to carry an 18 in. torpedo, its quiet-running Bristol Hercules sleeve-valve engines earned it the name 'Whispering Death'. With nose-mounted radar (known cryptically as RDF or 'magic mirrors' for security reasons), it was a highly effective night-fighter. Of equal importance to BACo was the fact that it appeared on the shop floor just in time to save the company from becoming a sub-contractor building the Short Stirling four-engined bomber. A total of 5,564 'Beaus' were built in the UK and a further 364 in Australia.

Meanwhile, enemy intelligence kept watch on Bristol Aeroplane's factories. Reconnaissance flights on 22 and 23 September 1940 revealed that No 501 Sqdn's Hurricanes had left Filton (to fight the Battle of Britain from RAF Kenley, Sussex). At 11.30a.m. on Wednesday 25 September 58 Heinkel III bombers with Messerschmitt 110 fighters struck. Over 100 tons of bombs fell on the site and surroundings. There were 281 casualties, 91 of which were killed when bombs hit shelters. A photograph taken during the raid by a Heinkel 111 of Kampfgeschwader 55 *Griefen* appears on page 72.

In February 1943 the first of another trio of twin-engined types flew. This was the Buckingham bomber – but it was too late to see service in World War Two. The second type was the Buckmaster trainer, which flew ten months later. It was used mainly to train pilots of the third type, the Brigand light ground attack bomber. It equipped RAF squadrons fighting terrorists in Malaya during 1950-54. Production of these three types totalled 382.

At the war's end, cancellation of military contracts focussed the directors' collective thoughts on finding alternative work for Bristol employees. They came up with pre-fabricated houses and hospitals, plastics, high quality cars and marine craft. Help was to come from another direction, too: the Brabazon Committee, named after its chairman, Lord Brabazon of Tara, a giant in British aviation. Its task was to consider future civil aircraft types required for trans-Atlantic, Empire and internal routes. Five were recommended: the Brabazon Type 1, a London-New York non-stop aeroplane, had priority. In March 1943 the job of building this aeroplane was given to BACo. It was to be a long one.

But first the company had to provide the means to do it. The design team was ready, but a new assembly building was required. And was the runway long enough? A huge eight-acre assembly hall was erected, but the runway caused many head and heart-aches. To extend it meant closing a new road and knocking down part of the village of Charlton which stood in the way. A Cabinet decision was required to enable this destructive project to proceed.

But while this 130-ton monster was being designed and built under the leadership of Leslie Frise, BACo needed more immediate work. This materialized in the shape of a 'no-frills' short-range general duty transport inspired, it is recorded, by the pre-war Bombay. Two versions were designed. The Freighter for cargo work, the Wayfarer for passengers. A total of 214 were built.

In 1947 Bristol's proposed Type 175 four-engined transport failed to meet exactly British Overseas Airways Corporation's requirements for a medium range airliner for its Empire routes. Neither did seven alternative designs by four other competitors. BOAC was choosey. But Bristol was nearest the mark. The Type 175, powered by four Bristol Proteus propeller-turbine engines and named Britannia, was ordered by BOAC. The prototype made its first flight on 16 August 1952 in the hands of Bill Pegg.

Britannia's flight development programme was not without some white-knuckle moments – including a forced landing in the mud of the Severn Estuary, happily without casualties. But things got better after that. The advertising catchphrase was 'Space, Pace and Grace'. The Britannia won airline markets around the world, its purring Proteus engines earning it the name 'Whispering Giant'. It served with the RAF too, where it won many hearts, but Britannia production was only eighty-five. Pure jet transports had won the day.

BACo's move into rotary-wing aircraft came in 1944. Its first helicopter was the Type 171, a single-rotor 4-5 seater which first flew on 27 July 1947. This launched the production of 178 Type 171s at the company's Old Mixon factory at Weston-super-Mare. Named Sycamore, they flew with the RAF and were exported. A handful were built for civil operators.

The second Hafner-designed Bristol helicopter, Type 173, with twin engines, twin rotors and thirteen seats, first flew in January 1952. Out of it came the RAF's Belvedere, but only twenty-six were produced. When deliveries began in March 1960 Bristol Helicopter Department had become the Bristol Helicopter Division of Westland Aircraft. This followed the Government's decision to centre all British helicopter-building interests on Westland at Yeovil.

Some five years earlier the company's project team had begun work on a supersonic transport project. This became the Type 223 with four underwing engines and a slender delta wing. The conceptual similarity between this Bristol design and France's Sud Aviation Super Caravelle was the basis of the Anglo-French collaboration agreement of 1962 which gave birth to Concorde.

Turbo-jet propulsion technology had been alive, reasonably well, and living in Rugby back in 1937. However, although BACo's turbo-prop studies began in 1940, it was 1946 before design studies for a jet engine for long range bombers began. But what an engine it became! The superb Olympus. Under the almost magical influence of Dr Stanley (later Sir Stanley) Hooker, who had joined the Company from Rolls-Royce in 1949, Bristol's engine development moved up several gears.

Across the Gloucester Road it took even longer for Type 188, the only wholly Bristol-designed and built jet aircraft, to fly. The date was 14 April 1962 and chief test pilot Godfrey Auty was – as they say – at the controls. This aeroplane, built for use in the Concorde research programme, was of stainless steel construction and designed to investigate kinetic heating of the airframe during sustained flight at twice sonic speed. Sadly, its de Havilland Gyron Junior engines gulped fuel so rapidly that the Type 188's flight time at full speed was too short to be of much value.

The second turbojet aircraft to carry a BACo Type number was the Type 221, in reality a much-modified Fairey FD.2. A one-time holder of the 1,132 m.p.h. world speed record, it probed the high speed handling characteristics of its Concorde-like ogee wing shape.

Other research and development programmes produced the Bloodhound ground-to-air guided missile for the RAF and for export, and the Red Rapier expendable bomber, which was abandoned in 1953.

As part of the Government's rationalization plans for the aircraft industry, British Aircraft Corporation was formed in June 1960, pooling Bristol's aviation interests with those of Vickers Ltd and the English Electric Company. Soon afterwards Hunting Aircraft Ltd was scooped up as well. Three and a half years later these four companies merged into a single unit, British Aircraft Corporation (Operating) Ltd, of which Bristol then became the Filton Division. Finally, in 1977, all but two of Britain's major aircraft companies merged to form British Aerospace. It is under that banner that aerospace work is carried on at Filton where, from 1910 until 1960, the skills of BCAC and BACo employees created some 16,000 aircraft and countless thousands of engines carrying the proud name of 'Bristol', the title which Sir George White had fought so hard to register for his company rather than use his own name. The Filton site and its products are the permanent memorial of this great Bristolian.

# Bristol's Engine Enterprise

Having bought the Cosmos Engineering Co of Fishponds in 1920, BCAC set up its aero-engine department, led by Roy Fedden, on 29 July. But outgoings were soon exceeding income, and the BCAC Board planned to close its new enterprise. Two months later the Jupiter II air-cooled radial engine became the first to pass the new severe Air Ministry type test, reaching 400 hp at 1,625 r.p.m. This saved the department's bacon. Shown at the 1921 Paris Air Show, the Jupiter knocked them flat and the French Gnome-Rhone company bought a licence to build it. The final accolade was an order for eighty-one engines for new RAF aircraft.

During the next decade, with the advance of technology, improved variants were regularly created. Seventeen foreign licence agreements were sold for the Jupiter and over 7,100 were built, powering some 260 different aircraft. Other 1920s engines included the Cherub, a 36 hp tiddler; Mercury, a compact 960 hp unit, and the big 1,065 Pegasus known universally as 'the Peggi'. This last pair were widely used during World War Two, the 'Peggi' spawning the Draco with its fuel injection. A technological leap forward was the sleeve-valve fitted in the Hydra, an unusual design with sixteen small cylinders in eight pairs with a common head. It tolled the death knell of poppet valves in BACo's engines. A series of sleeve-valved engines followed: the Perseus and Aquila, the twin-row (i.e. one row of cylinders staggered behind the other) fourteen-cylinder Hercules (fondly dubbed 'Herc'), the Taurus and, finally, the 2,520 hp Centaurus, the last of Bristol's great piston engines, which first ran in 1938. All these mainstream engines powered vast numbers of British and foreign aircraft for more than forty years.

Strangely, BACo appeared to ignore gas turbine engines until 1940, when it began design studies for a turbo-prop unit. But it was not until December 1946 that the Theseus, BACo's first turbo-prop was type tested. Later, four Theseus powered the Handley Page Hermes airliner. In 1944 work began on the 4,000 hp Proteus turbo-prop intended for the Brabazon and the Saunders-Roe Princess flying boat. It had a difficult six-year development programme despite being redesigned by Stanley Hooker, the chief engineer and Britain's outstanding engine guru. Fortunately for him and the engine, neither the Brabazon nor the Princess entered production. Instead the Proteus powered the Britannia airliner, flying millions of trouble-free hours.

Conversely, the Olympus turbojet, with a design thrust of 9,140 lb, was a superb engine from the moment it first ran in May 1950. Stanley Hooker proved this on the first run when he banged the throttle wide open to record a full 10,000 lb! Continuous 'tweaking' of this engine raised the thrust to 35,000 lb when first installed in Concorde, eventually reaching 40,000 lb (well, 39,940 lb to be honest) in service.

Bristol could also produce smaller jet engines, but, sadly, few received official support. However, the Orpheus was something else. It ran at 3,000 lb thrust in December 1954 and was eventually delivering some 5,800 lb. Thousands were produced by Bristol and licence-built in India, Italy and Germany.

In 1958 Stanley Hooker's team began design of the first vectored-thrust engine (the one with the swivelling jet pipes which gives the Harrier its 'get-up-and-go' performance) for fixed-wing vertical take-off aircraft. This became the Pegasus, which powers the Harrier/Sea Harrier/AV-8A and -8B family of VTOL aircraft built by British Aerospace and, in the USA, by McDonnell Douglas.

Then came a dramatic change of affairs at Filton. In 1959 Bristol Aero Engines (the company formed in 1956) and Armstrong Siddeley Motors merged to become Bristol-Siddeley Engines Ltd (BSEL). Then BSEL absorbed the de Havilland and Blackburn engine companies, Thus, Pegasus and other engines were developed and produced by BSEL until January 1968; then Rolls-Royce acquired BSEL, and the aero-engine plant at Filton became the Bristol Engine Division of Rolls-Royce. Thereafter, all engines being developed or in production were continued under the world renowned and revered two RRs badge of the great Rolls-Royce company.

# One
# In the Beginning

It was 1910, an era when aeroplanes were still regarded as the playthings of rich eccentrics or the obsessions of penniless inventors and engineers. It was born in a corrugated iron shed at the end of a four-mile tram ride from Bristol's city centre. It was the British and Colonial Aeroplane Co. Ltd, created by industrialist Sir George White Bt, a rich visionary obsessed with building aeroplanes.

We may never know what motivated him. Was it the desire to get a piece of the action in this new aerial adventure? Was it the great challenge which it presented? Getting more bums on the seats of the trams running out to Filton was certainly a bonus. Whatever it was, the British and Colonial Aeroplane Co. was different from many other aircraft companies who got into the business because they had good woodworking or other engineering skills or facilities for making things like wire netting, boats or lawn mowers. British and Colonial Aeroplane Co. was well financed and dedicated to the aviation business from the start. It never changed its mind.

Sir George White Bt, who in 1895 revolutionized the City of Bristol's transport systems, was the founder of the British and Colonial Aeroplane Co. (BCAC) at Filton in 1910.

These two iron sheds, leased from Bristol Tramways, were the cradle for the infant British and Colonial Aeroplane Company.

This Bristol Biplane, soon dubbed Boxkite, was between the 12th and 14th built, and numbered 12A. No customer would risk flying No. 13!

Boxkite production at Filton in about 1910. Note that all the workmen are wearing white 'chippies' aprons.

The 12th Boxkite was the first with extended upper wings. In January 1911 BCAC's French pilot Henri Jullerot took it to India, making numerous demonstration flights.

The Bristol Glider, which first flew on 17 December 1910, was built for Sir George White to present to the Bristol and West of England Aero Club of which he was President.

B for bicycles, bustles, a bowler hat – and Boxkite. As the pilot dips the petrol tank, the crew ignore the cavalry and public pressing close to their frail aeroplane on Durdham Downs, Bristol in 1911.

Filton, 1911. Sir George White (right) talks with an unidentified man, while a group of eager schoolboys watch a mechanic at work on a Boxkite.

The 1911 Racing Biplane was the first Bristol biplane with the 'tractor' layout, ie the engine is 'pulling' rather then 'pushing'. It crashed on its first attempt to fly in April 1911.

Collyns Pizey, an ex-Bristol Tramways apprentice, ran that company's generating station at the Counterslip, Bristol. Later he became an instructor on Boxkites at BCAC's Larkhill flying school.

The Bristol Monoplane was probably the first wholly-Bristol design. Two were built, one going to Russia to be shown in St Petersburg. Neither flew satisfactorily and they were abandoned.

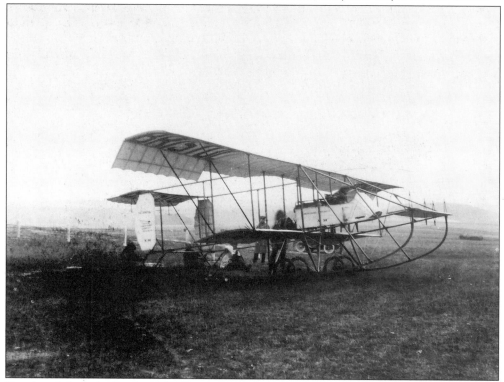

Developed from the Boxkite, the Type T Biplane was produced for the French pilot Maurice Tabuteau who flew it in the 1911 Circuit de l'Europe. Five were built.

Pierre Prier joined BCAC in June 1911. He designed a series of monoplanes, some of which were built for the War Office and some for export. This one went to Spain.

Designed by Eric Gordon England in 1912, this BCAC-built GE2 was the second of four undistinguished biplanes of similar configuration. GE3, built for Turkey, was not delivered.

Designed by Romanian Henri Coanda, this was the company's first production military monoplane. It was similar to those entered in the 1912 Larkhill Military Aeroplane Competition.

With a redesigned rudder, this Coanda monoplane was flown into third place by BCAC pilot Harry Busteed at the Larkhill Competition.

A trio of aviation pioneers at 'old' Filton House. From left are T.O.M. (later Sir Thomas) Sopwith, Sopwith Aviation's founder, Capt Bertram Dickson, BCAC's technical adviser, and Henri Coanda, its *chef technique*.

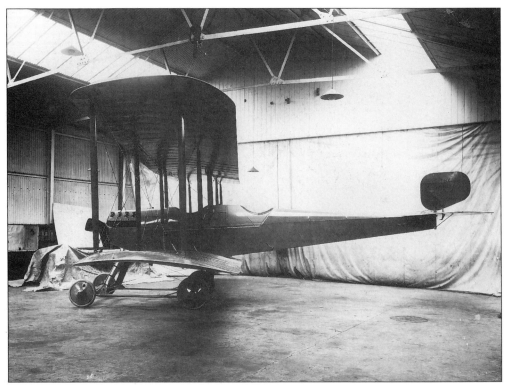

Seven of these Coanda-designed BR.7 biplanes were built at Filton and one in Germany. The four wheels gave it stability during take-off, landing and taxiing on rough airfields.

The 1912 Burney X2 was boat and aeroplane. Being water-tight, it floated. Driven by water screws at speed, as seen here, hydrofoils on legs raised it out of the water. The airscrew was then engaged and, in theory, the whole contraption took-off.

The Baby which grew up to be a Scout. No 206, the original Baby Biplane – or Scout – at BCAC's Brooklands site in 1914, where pilot Harry Busteed prepares to fly it.

Lord Carbery paid BCAC £400 for this modified Scout A – minus an engine. Here he starts from Hendon in the London-Manchester Air Race in July 1914.

Two

# The War to End Wars

When the Kaiser's War came in August 1914, Britain was ill-prepared to mount air operations against the German Navy or in support of the British Expeditionary Force on mainland Europe. The infant Royal Flying Corps, barely three years old, went to France with a motley bunch of aeroplanes, none officially carrying guns or bombs. Filton-built BE.2s, designed by the Royal Aircraft Factory, were certainly among them.

But things changed. British and Colonial Aeroplane Co. set up another factory at Brislington and designed and built substantial numbers of Scouts and M.1 monoplanes for the RFC and the Royal Naval Air Service. These were followed by the F.2A and F.2B Bristol Fighter. By the war's end four years later, the Royal Air Force, itself only seven months old following its formation on 1 April 1918, was the world's most powerful air service, supplied by a vast, efficient aircraft industry.

Frank Barnwell in RAF uniform. His fertile brain produced a steady flow of innovative designs from 1911 until he died in an air crash in 1938.

An early flying test bed. This Scout D had a French Clerget engine for which Frank Barnwell designed an enormous hemispherical propeller spinner intended for the later M.1A monoplane.

Sailor in the snow. A Royal Naval Air Service Scout D taxies in, with help from two running ground crew, at an unidentified airfield.

These overalled and mob-capped ladies worked in BCAC's wing shop during WW1. Fifth from right in the front row is Lillian Norman, who met her future husband on top of a Bristol Tramways tramcar travelling to work!

The first of two S.2A two-seat fighters, in which the crew sat cosily side-by-side in the single cockpit, at Filton in 1917. It was nicknamed 'Tubby' because of its girth.

They called it the TTA – Twin Tractor A – because its twin propellers pulled instead of pushed from behind. The two crew had three machine guns. Only two TTAs were built.

A new F.2A two-seat fighter, built at the company's Brislington factory and powered by a 190 hp Rolls-Royce Falcon, stands ready for delivery.

The F.2B Bristol Fighter – the 'Brisfit' – was the RFC's most successful World War One two-seater fighter. This one, seen at Baginton airfield, Coventry in 1961, was the last flying example of 5,308 built.

Bristol F.2B Fighter production during the 1917-18 era.

This dual-control Bristol Fighter is seen during its service with Oxford University Air Squadron in 1930.

Wolf in sheep's clothing No. 1. G-ADJR, a civil-registered ex-RFC F.2B. The engine cowling carries the words 'London Film Productions. Camera Ship'.

A single-seat fighter, the M.1 was designed in 1916. Its top speed was 132 m.p.h. but a 50 m.p.h. landing speed ruled out its use from Western Front airfields. Instead, the RFC flew it in the Middle East.

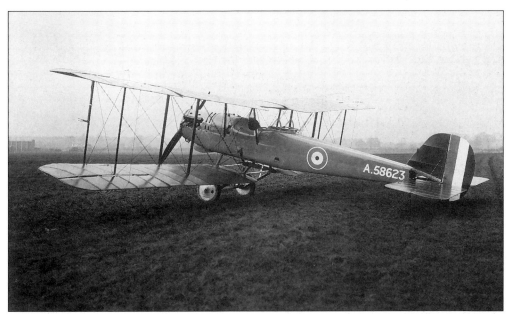

The first of two all-metal MR.1 two-seat reconnaissance aircraft built at Filton in 1918. Its metal wings were built by the Steel Wing Co. at Gloucester.

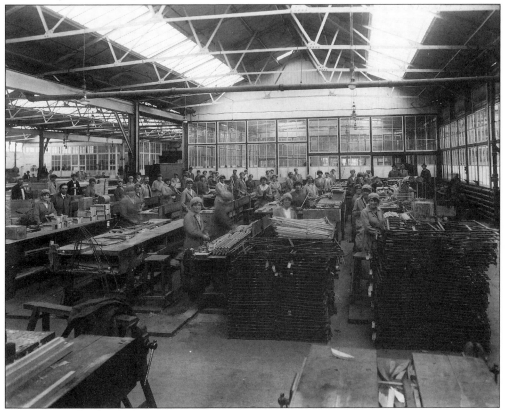

This 1918 photograph of the woodworking department shows the effect of war on the workforce. Most of them are women replacing the younger men who went to war.

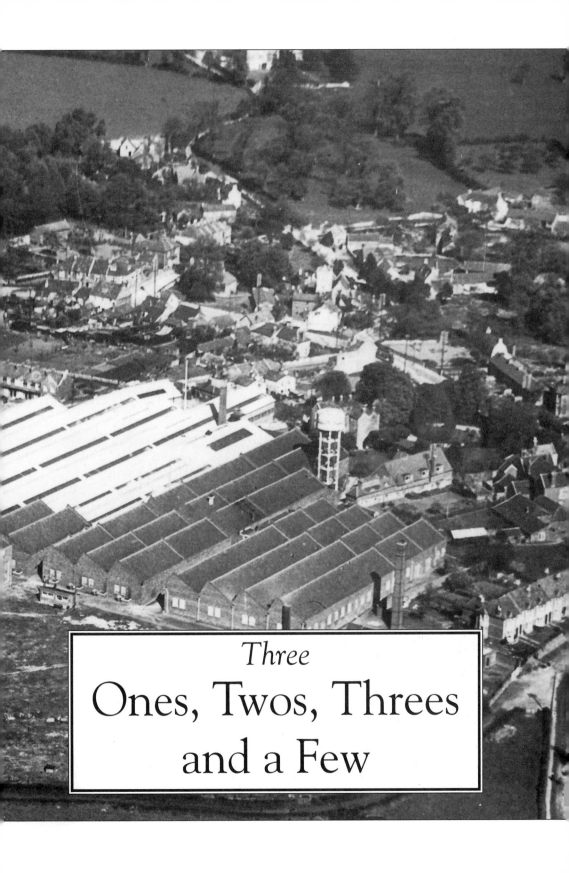

# Three
# Ones, Twos, Threes and a Few

When peace broke free again in November 1918, the cessation of military orders left dozens of companies in the aviation business in a parlous state. Fortunately, British and Colonial Aeroplane Co. got a stay of execution on F.2B Fighter orders and experimental contracts. In 1920 the picture looked bleak for the company's new aero-engine department, but then its Jupiter engine won orders. It was a close-run thing. Then came the name change. Now it was the Bristol Aeroplane Co.

There was, however, a succession of designs which progressed no further than the wastepaper basket. If any did spark off actual cutting of wood or metal, they were built only in penny numbers. There were, too, some non-aviation products for the commercial and private road vehicle manufacturers, including a brace of Bristol Monocars, single-seat light cars which didn't enter production. It was all skin-of-the-teeth survival.

A triple hangar block at Patchway in 1919. The Gloucester Road crosses behind it. Hayes Lane to Charlton goes left from the crossroads, and Gipsy Patch Lane goes directly opposite to the top of the picture.

During 1919-20 BCAC built 168 Parnall Panther naval aircraft under sub-contract. They could fold in half for snug stowage in aircraft carriers.

They nicknamed it 'Brock' and 'Barnwell's Week-ender'. This is the 1919 Badger designed by Barnwell to replace the F.2B Fighter, but its dodgy ABC Dragonfly engine spoilt any chance of a production order.

In 1921 the Jupiter II was the first to pass a severe new type-test. The valve pushrods automatically compensated for cylinder expansion when hot. Some 7,100 were built for over 260 different aircraft types.

Jupiter production at Bristol Aeroplane Company (BACo) in the early 1920s. In front are two three-cylinder Lucifers engines, one fitted with its exhaust collector ring.

The Braemar II bomber seen in 1919. Note the four-wheel undercarriage and the four US Liberty engines in paired 'push-me-pull-you' layout on the centre wings.

Sheep in wolf's clothing No. 2. This big 1922 Pullman 'airliner' was a converted Braemar bomber. Pilots hated it and carried axes in case a quick exit was needed in an emergency! It never carried passengers.

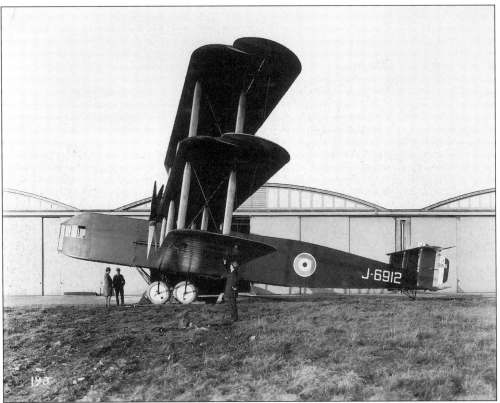

The two 1921 Tramp triplanes cost £23,000 each to build. Their four engines, in a fuselage 'engine room', drove two propellers through gearboxes and transmission shafts. Neither of them flew.

Derived from the F.2B Fighter, the Tourer carried two passengers seated side-by-side behind the pilot. Thirty-three Tourers were built, and this one, with a coupe top, was one of a number sold in the USA.

Three single-seat Babes were built – two biplanes and a monoplane. Intended for private ownership, lack of a reliable small engine meant that only one of the biplanes ever flew, in November 1919.

Built as a test-bed for the Cosmos Jupiter engine and as a racer, the Bullet was a success in both roles. It test flew Jupiters, and gained good results – though never winning – in air races between 1920 and 1924.

The Seely, seen at Filton in 1920, was built to boost safety and comfort in civil aircraft. Developed from the Tourer, it carried two passengers but in a more comfortable enclosed cabin.

The Bristol Ten-seaters, of which three were built, were flown by Instone Airways, Handley Page Transport Ltd and Imperial Airways during 1922-26.

Ambulance with wings. The sole military Ten-seater, named Brandon, first flew in 1924. It served on ambulance duties from RAF Halton for several years from 1925.

Yet another example of a Bristol two-in-one aeroplane was the 1923 Bullfinch. Three were built, two as unusually-configured single-seat parasol monoplane fighters ...

... and one, a year later, as a two-seat biplane reconnaissance aircraft. Neither of these Bullfinches was ordered for the Royal Air Force.

A reconditioned M.1B military scout, the M.ID was civil-registered G-EAVP in September 1920. It won several major air races before crashing in flames in the Grosvenor Cup Race on 23 June 1923.

A World War One song, 'Pack up your troubles...' had a line which went, 'While you've a Lucifer (i.e. match) to light your fag, smile, boys...' This candelabra, made from a Lucifer engine which hung in Buckland Old Mill, Sir Roy Fedden's home, would certainly have caused some smiles.

G-EBEW, the first of three Lucifer-powered Taxiplanes built, seen at Filton in 1923. It carried two passengers side-by-side in the rear cockpit.

This photograph reveals the close physical integration of BACo with the Filton community in the 1920s. Factory buildings on the city side are cheek-by-jowl with houses. The ones in the middle are in Fairlawn Avenue.

Flying Barrel. The Racer, its engine buried inside its fuselage, was a rare sight in the sky in July 1922, flying only seven times. The undercarriage was retracted by a chain and sprocket gear.

The 1924 Bloodhound two-seat fighter failed to win orders, but it proved the Jupiter engine's reliability to Imperial Airways top brass with a long distance flight to Cairo and a series of UK flights.

The Berkeley two-seat bomber of 1924, with a Rolls-Royce Condor engine, was one of only a handful of Bristol types built between 1920 and 1947 not to have a Bristol engine.

'Contact'. Hand swinging the two-seat Brownie II's 36 hp Cherub engine was not too arduous. Three Brownies were built in 1924. Registered G-EBJK, 'JL and 'JM, BACo pilots instantly named them 'Jack', 'Jill' and 'Jim'.

The 1925 Type 92 Laboratory Biplane was the least known of the company's aeroplanes. It flight tested full-size engine cowlings to compare data obtained with wind-tunnel models.

Viva el Boarhound! This 1925 two-seat fighter received the thumbs-down from the RAF because its handling characteristics were poor. But two were sold to Mexico in 1928.

The Beaver was a modified and more handsome Boarhound with improvements designed to correct the latter's faults which had been identified by RAF pilots. Sadly, they still rejected it.

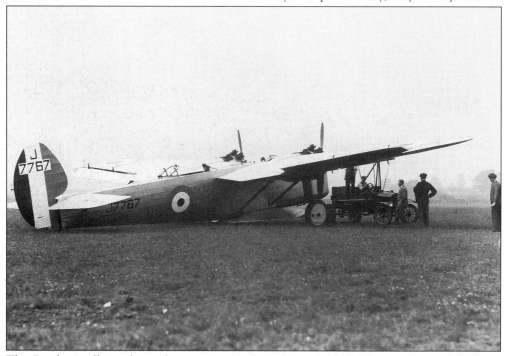

The Bagshot's all-metal cantilever wing owed much to the little Brownie's wing. Sadly, it twisted in flight, so this big twin-engined two-seat fighter was abandoned in 1931.

Designed as a racer/test bed, the 1926 Badminton, with each engine cylinder 'helmeted', was modified to suit its dual roles. It crashed on test for the 1927 King's Cup Race.

A simply-equipped two-seat fighter, the Type 101 was spurned by the Air Ministry because of its partly wooden structure. It broke up in flight in November 1929 when a metal fitting failed.

One of the eighty-three Armstrong Whitworth Siskin IIIA fighters built by BACo during 1928-30. It carries No. 19 Squadron's blue and white chequerboard markings.

Final assembly of air-cooled radial engines, possibly Mercuries, in the aero-engine department during the 1930s. There are eighteen engines visible and thirty-three men working on them.

Rows of belt-driven Alfred Herbert lathes in No. 1 machine shop in the 1930s. The designers of numerically-controlled machining centres were still 'mewling and puking in their mothers' arms'.

The unmarked Bulldog I second prototype seen at Filton with the smaller rudder as used on the first aeroplane. This was subsequently enlarged to improve handling characteristics in a spin.

No doubting who ran the RAF's Reserve Flying School at Filton in 1931. On the airfield are three Bristol Primary Training Machines and a two-seat Blackburn Bluebird.

The Mercury, a more svelte power unit than the earlier Jupiter, had enclosed valve gear and other performance-enhancing devices. Total production was 21,993 engines.

Jupiter and Mercury engines on test stands with two and four blade propellers.

Entente Cordiale. Bulldog II, G-ABAC, with a French-built Gnome-Rhone Jupiter. Englishmen R. Ninnes, N. Rowbotham and K. Bartlett (later Bristol directors) headed Gnome-Rhone's 1920s aero-engine team.

September 1935. Bulldog II, G-ABBB, test flew the Aquila sleeve-valve engine. It went to the Science Museum in 1939, but in 1957 was made airworthy for the Shuttleworth Trust.

Chief test pilot Godfrey Auty prepares to fly the restored Jupiter-engined Bulldog, G-ABBB, at Filton on 22 June 1961. Note the vintage leather helmet and knee-pad he is carrying.

In January 1930 these eight Bulldogs went 'down under' to the Royal Australian Air Force. At the far end is the sole, and later abandoned, Type 110A five-seater intended for Australian airlines.

Bristol design office staff with Swedish Air Force pilots during the 1930s. Back row, from the left: Leslie Frise, who became chief designer and engineer, Freddy Coles, -?-, Mickey Dunn, W.B. MacKenzie. Front row: Kaptin ?, W.A. Servil, H.W. Dunn, -?-, -?-.

The sole Bullpup failed to win orders but flight tested four Bristol engines. Flown here by C.A. Washer at the 1935 SBAC Show, it had an Aquila engine, Dowty undercarriage and low pressure 'doughnut' tyres.

This 1931 Type 118 was a two-seat general purpose 'do-it-all' aeroplane for the RAF – then the Air Ministry moved the goal posts. Barnwell changed it a bit, fitted a gun turret and – hey presto! – the Type 120.

The Type 123 was BACo's first offering for the F.7/30 fighter competition. The preferred Rolls-Royce Goshawk steam-cooled engine had too many question marks hanging over it for ultimate success.

Type 133, BACo's Mercury-engined entry in the F.7/30 competition. Test pilot T.W. Campbell left the undercarriage down when spinning it. He baled out when it wouldn't stop spiralling earthwards into Longwell Green.

Designed in Bristol, built in Belfast and named Bombay. Too big for Filton's hangars to swallow, fifty of these 96 ft span bomber/transports were made by Short and Harland.

Bombay production by Short and Harland in 1939. The multiplicity of wooden steps and staging and the bunting are the interesting features of this photograph.

The two figures by the Bombay's undercarriage give scale to this big aeroplane. Hurricane fighters of No. 501 Auxiliary Air Force Squadron based at Filton are in the left background.

In 1935 Bristol won sub-contract orders for 141 Hawker Audax army co-operation aircraft like this Hawker-built example. All were delivered during the first seven months of 1936.

In 1936 this Pegasus-powered Type 130A was specially created to regain the world's altitude record from the Italians. On 28 September Sqdn Ldr F.D.R. Swain flew it to 49,967 ft to set a new record.

Type 142 was a high speed private aircraft built during 1934-5 for Lord Rothermere, the *Daily Mail*'s owner. Named *Britain First*, it was 50 m.p.h. faster than the RAF's fighters!

Type 142, showing the wing section, Mercury engine nacelle and mounting structure, and the Dowty 'nutcracker' undercarriage retracting mechanism.

The Type 143, a slightly enlarged Type 142 with Bristol Aquila engines, stands on display in the 29 June 1936 SBAC Show at Hendon.

This rare photograph shows the prototype Blenheim light bomber in flight on 25 June 1936. Note the retracted tailwheel which was later locked down because retracting it did not increase speed.

After Finland had bought twenty-eight Blenheim Is and IVs in 1936, the Finnish company Valtion Lentokonetehdas licence-built forty-five Blenheim Is at Tampere. This is the twenty-eighth off the line.

An early crop of Blenheims. Final assembly of some of the first batch of 150 Blenheim Is seen on 4 August 1937 awaiting delivery of their Bristol dorsal gun turrets.

The crew of a Blenheim I of No. 44 Sqdn, based at RAF Waddington, prepare for a flight on 13 July 1938. This aircraft was the 100th Blenheim built at Filton.

Four
World War II

The year 1934 signalled the start of numerous RAF expansion schemes culminating in Scheme M which increased its strength to 3,550 first line 'teeth' aircraft and to 9,343 in all. Some aviation savants thought the programme was two years too late. But aviation technology was advancing rapidly. Had rearmament begun two years earlier, RAF squadrons could have been lumbered with fleets of biplanes. Instead retractable undercarriages, cantilever monoplane wings, metal structures and supercharged engines had arrived on the aircraft scene.

Bristol Aeroplane Company's designers and production engineers took full advantge of these new technologies. The factories and their workforces were vastly increased in size and throughout the War years they poured out a never-ending stream of military aircraft and engines for the Allied Air Forces.

A Blenheim I of No. 211 Sqdn lands at Tatoi/Menidi airfield in Greece after attacking Italian positions in Albania during November 1940.

'Now, don't drop it.' A crew member of a No. 11 Sqdn Blenheim I hands a camera to a waiting ground crewman at Ma'aten Bagush in the Western Desert during August 1940.

A line-up of a dozen of the 15 Bolingbroke IV-Ws, produced by Fairchild Aircraft at Longueuil, for the Royal Canadian Air Force. Fairchild built 676 Bolingbrokes between 1939 and 1943.

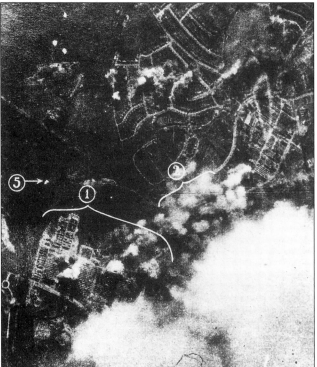

BACo's factories, 21 February 1937. Gipsy Patch factory is lower left, Rodney Works centre. Blenheims share the airfield with No. 501 Sqdn's Harts and Tiger Moths. Note the road roundabout in the lower right corner.

Having discovered that No. 501 Sqdn's Hurricanes had gone from Filton, the Luftwaffe bombed BACo factories on 25 September 1940. (See page 10.) Note the road roundabout in the lower left corner. This photograph was taken by one of the Heinkel III bombers.

A gaggle of Blenheim IVs – possibly from No. 15 Sqdn – up from RAF Wyton in 1940.

A Rootes Securities-built Blenheim IV of No. 18 Sqdn which fought in France during 1940. Note the guns in the dorsal turret and the rearward firing unit under the nose.

'Well, let's get on with it.' The crew of a No. 88 Sqdn Blenheim IV climb aboard their aircraft for an early morning take-off from RAF Attlebridge, Norfolk in October 1941.

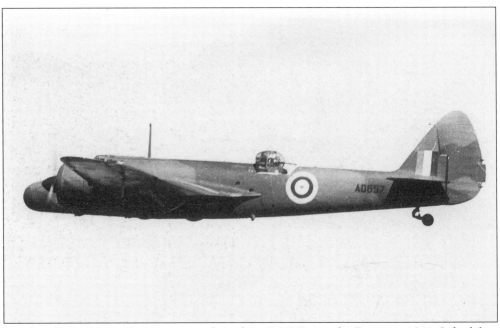

The first Bisley I ground support aircraft up from RAF Boscombe Down in 1941. It had four nose-mounted .303 in. Browning guns. Renamed Blenheim V, Rootes built 942.

Most of a Beaufighter and a rubbish bin (right foreground) plus bags of Beaufort and Beaufighter fuselages in a final assembly shop in March 1941.

'Do not turn' reads the chalked message on the port propeller blades of this Beaufort I at Boscombe Down. A mystery aeroplane, it was converted to an experimental transport.

An intrepid photographer got this close-up view of a No. 217 Sqdn Beaufort I landing at Leuchars in Spring 1942.

Tin fish aplenty. RAF ground crew of No. 22 Sqdn line up a selection of air-launched torpedoes ready for their Beaufort Is at an airfield 'somewhere in England'.

Sir Roy Fedden with some of the 1921 aero engine department staff photographed in about 1942. Left to right are S. Damsell, R.N. Swinchatt, ? Brown, ? Gulliford, W. Stammers, F. Powell, H. Wills, -?-, R. Williams, Fedden, ? Cox, A.G. Adams, ? Bennett, L.F. 'Bunny' Butler, A. Houlson, ? Collett, ? O'Gorman.

Filton, 17 July 1939. The prototype of some 5,900 Beaufighters which were eventually built. Royal Observer Corps members described the Beaufighter as 'two ruddy great engines hotly pursued by an airframe'.

'Night's black agents to their preys do rouse,' as Shakespeare might have said of this No. 604 Sqdn Beaufighter I night fighter – if he'd been at RAF Middle Wallop in September 1940.

The Hercules twin-row 14-cylinder sleeve-valve power unit, 'the ruddy great engines' which powered almost all Beaufighter variants, produced some 1,700 hp.

Rolls-Royce Merlin engines powered 450 Beaufighter IIFs when Hercules deliveries slowed. This one flew with No. 406 Royal Canadian Air Force Sqdn, whose motto was 'We kill by night'. They did.

The one-off Beaufighter with two 1,720 hp Griffon engines was used as a Rolls-Royce test bed at Hucknall.

One of 2,095 Beaufighter X anti-shipping strike aircraft built. A No. 455 Royal Australian Air Force Sqdn aircraft, it carried four 20 mm cannon, plus a torpedo or rockets, and was fitted with nose-mounted radar.

'What shall we hit 'em with Skipper? A few rockets, some cannon fire, the tin-fish or shall we give 'em a full house?' The crew of a Beaufighter discuss tactics before an anti-shipping strike.

An Australian-built Beaufighter of the Royal Australian Air Force over Melbourne in 1945. The 'Beau's' fast, almost silent approach to enemy ground targets earned it the soubriquet 'The Whispering Death'.

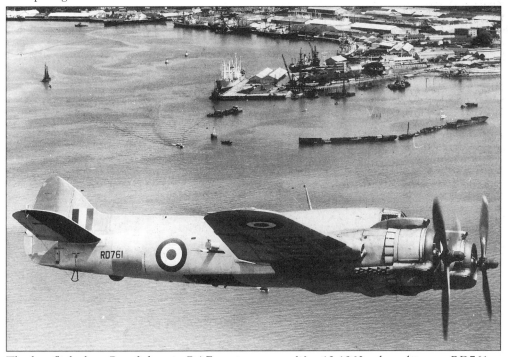

The last flight by a Beaufighter in RAF service was on May 12 1960, when this one, RD761, a target-towing variant, made its final trip from RAF Seletar, Malaya.

The second prototype Buckingham 1 bomber at Filton in April 1943. Note the new Bristol B.XII dorsal gun turret and the underfuselage bomb aimer's 'bath' with its B.XIII turret.

Students and staff of the No. 1 Course of the Empire Test Pilots School visited BACo in September 1943. Among BACo people they met were Bill Pegg, test pilot (front row, centre), I. Llewellyn Owen (extreme left, middle row) and Eric Swiss, test pilot (back row, centre). Wing Commander Sammy Wroath, ETPS Commandant, is on Pegg's right.

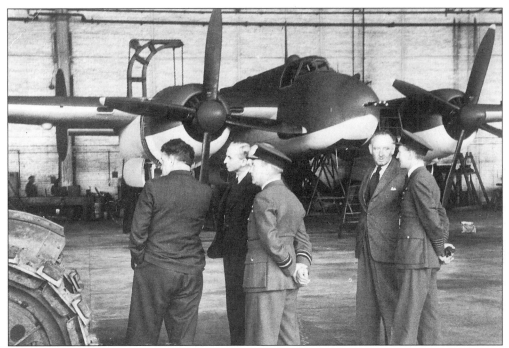

Buckmaster and VIPs in 1944. From the left are Harold Pollard, pioneer of high-tensile steel strip construction, Sir Archibald Sinclair, Air Minister, A.E. 'Russ' Russell, chief designer, an unidentified Air Vice Marshal, H. Thomas and Group Captain H. Stringer, MAP Overseer at Filton.

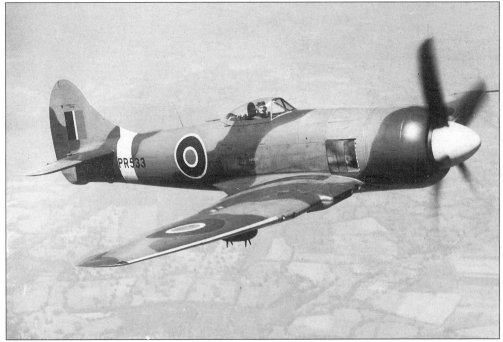

Fifty Hawker Tempest II fighter-bombers, like this Hawker-built example, were produced by BACo's Filton and Old Mixon factories during 1945-46.

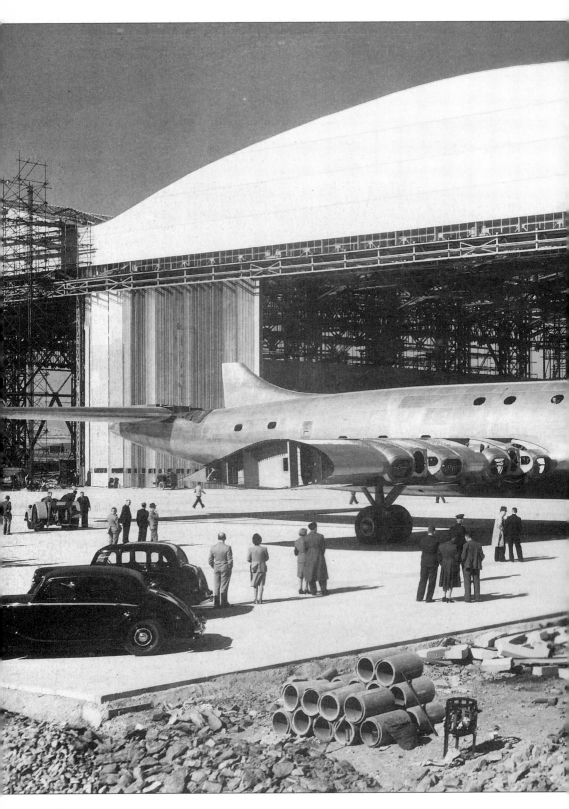

*Five*
# Peace, Imperfect Peace

In 1945, for the second time in a little over twenty-five years, Britain's aircraft industry had to adjust to peacetime markets. (BACo kept its workers busy making high quality cars, prefabricated houses and plastic products.) Earlier, in February 1943, a committee chaired by the redoubtable Lord Brabazon of Tara had recommended the types of civil aircraft needed in the post-war period.

It listed five types ranging from the Brabazon Type 1, a trans-Atlantic non-stop express airliner, to the Type 5, a small six/eight-seater for internal services. After being omitted from companies chosen to tender for contracts, the job of building the Type 1 was given to Bristol. It turned out to be the company's biggest white elephant. There were the Freighter and Britannia, however, to cushion the blow.

A Buckmaster from the Empire Flying School.

Ordered as Buckinghams but built as Buckmasters, this pristine example, seen at Filton in 1949, was one of a production batch of 100.

The prototype Brigand T.4 radar trainer was a converted bomber variant in 1949. It is surrounded by a motley collection of Ansons, Dakotas, a Heron and a Vampire.

Horace King (right), Bristol's stress engineer and structural trouble-shooter, discusses a Brigand problem with an unidentified RAF Squadron Leader and a civilian in Malaya.

Three Brigands, possibly from No. 84 Sqdn, in stepped-up echelon. Note all three crew members grouped in one large cockpit – or is it a flight deck?

PROTOTYPE T.170.                                        NO NEG No.

The prototype Type 170 was a flying six-ton truck designed for quick production when peace broke out in 1945. Two versions were produced: the cargo-carrying Freighter and the people-moving Wayfarer.

Bristol's first gas turbine engine was the Theseus, which first ran on 18 July 1945. Four of these 2,000 shp turbo-props powered the Handley Page Hermes V airliners.

*Bristol A/c Neg T170/20*

'Open wide.' A freighter opens its nose doors to swallow one of the two cars it could carry. The presence of snow on the airfield explains the fur collar on the car driver's coat.

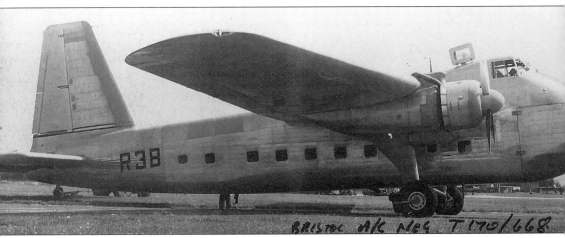

*Bristol A/c Neg T170/668*

The second of two Freighter XIs built, this went to Suidair International in South Africa in August 1947. Returned to BACo, it flew, registered R38, until converted to a Mk 21.

A collapsed starboard undercarriage in snowy conditions put a temporary halt to operations for CF-WAE, a Canadian-registered Wayfarer.

Why was a Silver City Airways' Wayfarer disgorging a motor cycle, a Bentley, an unidentifiable 'flop top' and umpteen passengers? For a publicity photograph. The motor cycle is on its stand!

'Fill her up, please.' This Freighter 31M of No. 41 Sqdn Royal New Zealand Air Force, appears to have stopped for petrol at a filling station. In fact, it is being serviced at RAF Changi in 1953.

Registered F-BKBI and named *Onze Novembre*, this Freighter Mk 32 of Companie Air Transport unloads passengers and cars at Le Touquet Airport.

*BRISTOL A/c NEG T170/1997*

Best known to the travelling public were, perhaps, Silver City Airways' Super Freighters and Super Wayfarers. Five feet longer than earlier versions, they could carry three cars.

One of the 11,250 prefabricated aluminium houses built by Bristol Aeroplane Co. at the Banwell and Old Mixon factories during 1945-47. Some are still in use in Bristol.

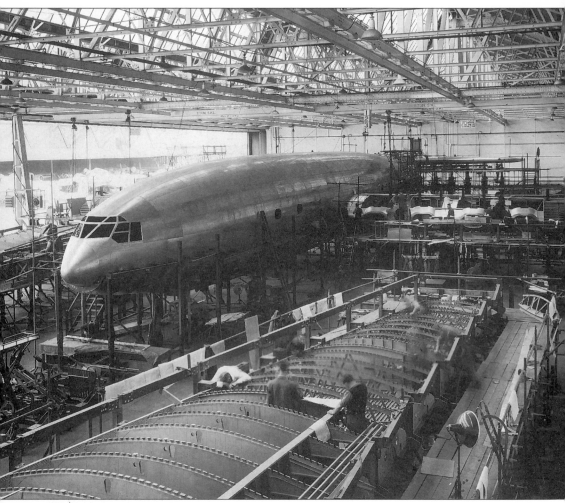

The first Type 167 Brabazon fuselage and wings take material shape in Filton's No. 2 Flight Shed during early 1947.

The very snug fit of the Brabazon fuselage inside No. 2 Flight Shed prevented completion of the tail unit until it could be removed from its jigs and towed to larger premises!

On 4 October 1947 the Brabazon was moved out of No. 2 Flight Shed. It emerged backward, urged on by a tractor, with the white overalled ground crew manually steering the nosewheel.

'Ah – that's better.' Having been towed backwards half a mile to the still unfinished final erection hall – fondly dubbed the 'Brab Hangar' – the first Brabazon waits in the sunshine to go in.

With four – yes, four – of its engines running in the starboard wing, the only completed example of the Brabazon undergoes ground checks at Filton in the summer of 1949.

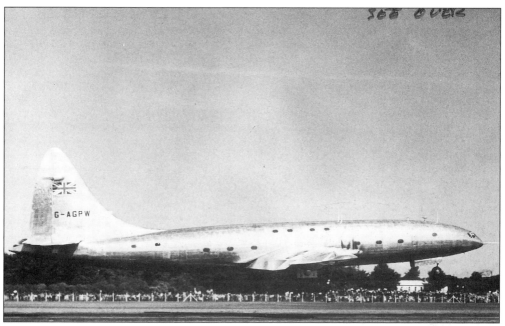

Filton, Sunday 4 September 1949. The Brabazon, proudly carrying the Union flag on its fin, gets airborne in the hands of Bill Pegg, BACo's recently appointed chief test pilot.

Men with hats. Bill Pegg (extreme left), A.E. Russell, chief designer, (hands clasped) and Sir Reginald Verdon Smith, chairman, (extreme right) with VIP visitors – and the Brabazon.

The mighty Brabazon was a pioneer on a grand scale. Its majestic splendour is well portrayed in this view of the aeroplane taken during its visit to London Heathrow Airport on 16 June 1950.

Two pairs of Hercules engines, delivering 10,000 hp, drove two pairs of propellers – each rotating in opposite directions – in each Brabazon wing.

Almost as long as three cricket pitches (177 ft), and with wings spanning 230 ft, the mighty Brabazon dwarfs the attendant Freighter.

Making its second appearance at the SBAC Display at Farnborough, the Brabazon, with a new multi-wheel undercarriage, approaches over Cody's Tree and the Black Sheds in September 1950.

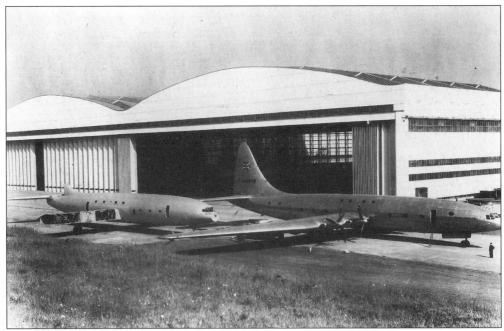

The first Brabazon with the unfinished second aircraft. Axed (literally!) mainly for political and financial reasons rather than because of technical failure, they were broken up in October 1953.

A Bristol 403, introduced in 1953, outside the old Filton House. It was one of a range of sporting saloons built to aircraft standards by the company from 1946 until 1961.

An early 1950s scene at Filton where some of BOAC's Lockheed Constellations and Boeing Stratocruisers are undergoing major overhauls in the airlines' service base.

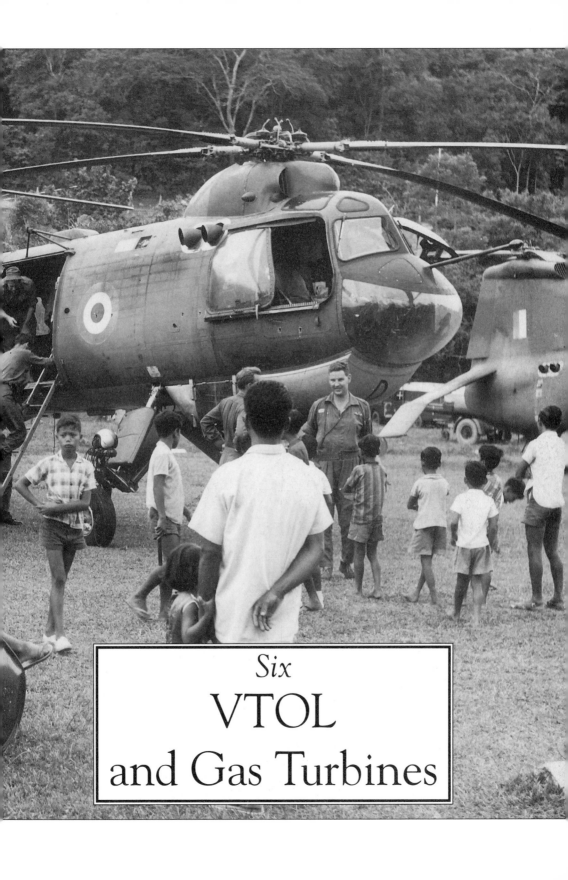

*Six*

# VTOL
# and Gas Turbines

In its final years Bristol Aeroplane Company's factories at Filton and Weston-super-Mare were involved in two distinct forms of VTOL aeroplanes: rotary wing helicopters and the Pegasus vectored-thrust engine for the Harrier family of fixed-wing VTOL aircraft.

Possibly to the delight of local residents, jet propulsion was late arriving on the Filton scene. Although a four-jet bomber project was unsuccessfully proposed as early as 1946, it was April 1962 before the first wholly Bristol-designed and built jet aircraft got airborne. By then British Aircraft Corporation had scooped up about a third of Britain's aircraft companies and the name Bristol Aeroplane Co disappeared. Finally, in 1977, to satisfy a Labour Government, the industry was nationalized and, with just a few exceptions, British Aerospace plc acquired virtually all of the rest.

Outside looking in. The large 'bay window' in the Type 171 helicopter cabin gave the pilot an excellent forward and downward view.

Inside looking out. Like the inside of an early Morris Minor, the Sycamore's cockpit seems sparsely equipped. The car-sized wipers clear only a small part of the rain-spattered windscreen.

A BACo machine shop decorated with bunting and Union flags to celebrate – what? Possibly Her Majesty The Queen's Coronation in 1953. The girls' smiling faces suggest a happy occasion.

'All work and no play No. 1.' During the 1950s interdepartmental competitions were popular. The Filton Drawing Office XI won the 1952 Football Trophy. Front row, from the left, in suits, are Don Waterman, A.E. (later Sir Archibald) Russell, Fred Symonds, and Ron Ellison, with captain Les Mealing in the centre.

Type 171 helicopter over the 'vasty wastes of Severn's waters'. G-AMWI had varied roles: BACo's trainer for German pilots, it was bought by the Royal Australian Navy, then sold for crop-spraying.

Peter (later Sir Peter) Masefield, Bristol Aircraft's managing director, (right) with Edward 'Ted' Bowyer, Society of British Aircraft Constructors' Director, during his visit to BACo on 12-13 May 1958.

The military Type 171 was the first British-designed helicopter to serve in the RAF. This one was the first used for search and rescue by Fighter Command.

The first two of fifty Sycamore 52s built at Weston for the German Federal Government. They were used by German forces for ambulance, air-sea rescue, and transport duties.

Built for the Royal Australian Navy, this Sycamore HR.50 has a taller undercarriage, a hydraulic winch, and what is believed to be a roll-up canvas door with side zip fastners.

Ground troops approach a Sycamore of No. 110 Sqdn RAF in a jungle clearing during the Brunei campaign in 1964.

The last RAF Sycamore flies over London and Belfast simultaneously. How so? HMS Belfast is the warship moored near London's Tower Bridge.

C.T.D. 'Sox' Hosegood, BACo's chief helicopter test pilot, hovers the prototype Type 173 in August 1952. Designed as a 13-seat people-mover and dubbed 'Rotorcoach', it never entered service.

The second Type 173 in British European Airways markings also carries RAF roundels and serial number XH379. The poor thing didn't know whether it was a civilian or an airman.

'Which is the sharp end, sailor?' 'Sox' Hosegood leans out of the prototype Type 173 helicopter during sea trials in the aircraft carrier HMS Eagle in 1953.

An experimental tail unit on XH379. Note the wool tufts on the outrigged fin to check airflow around it.

A pre-production Type 192 Belvedere, XG451, the military development of the Type 173, with four-blade rotors and interim undercarriage. Here it lifts a Bristol-Ferranti Bloodhound guided missile and trolley.

'Up you come.' A No. 66 Sqdn RAF Belvedere of the Far East Air Force hoists a partly dismantled Westland Whirlwind HAR 4 using its external strop.

A trio of RAF Belvederes in stepped-up port echelon formation over South Gloucestershire.

Young Malayans chat to the crews of a pair of No. 66 Sqdn Belvederes during a casualty evacuation operation in the jungle.

The sign which says it all. No. 66 Squadron's Belvederes were dubbed 'flying longhouses' by the local population in Borneo, many of whom lived in the communal longhouses typical of that area.

Bill Pegg taxies G-ALBO, the first prototype Britannia, using only two of its Bristol Proteus turbo-prop engines. When Britannias entered service in February 1957, jet airliners were already breathing down their necks.

Two Vickers Valiant 'V'-bombers of No. 49 Sqdn RAF (left) and one from No. 207 Sqdn seen at Filton for modification by BACo engineers during the early 1960s.

Proteus power for prototype G-ALBO ... and for all the eighty-four Britannias which followed it. However, G-ALBO did test-fly a single Orion engine in its port outer nacelle in August 1956.

G-ALBO at Farnborough in 1952. In 1954 it was nearly lost after partial flap failure flipped it onto its back. Only superior airmanship by pilot Walter Gibb enabled control to be regained.

Bristol power for Cuba. Smooth, quiet-running Proteus turbo-prop engines won the Britannia a new name – the 'Whispering Giant'.

The Dowty four-wheel bogey type main undercarriage fitted to all variants of the Britannia. The pattern of the tyre treads is interesting.

SPH NEG 5.5.89 (BMN)

On 4 February 1954 an engine in the second prototype Britannia disintegrated in flight and caught fire. Bill Pegg opted to belly-land on the Severn's mud flats. There were no casualties but the rising tide submerged G-ALRX. It was recovered and written off.

G-ANBA, the first production Britannia in BOAC markings, landing at Filton. It first flew in September 1954. After some 650 hours development flying it entered BOAC service in 1957.

'All work and no play No. 2.' Bristol executives and their ladies at the 1957 Design Office Ball. From left are -?-, Admiral Sir Matthew Slattery, chairman, and Lady Slattery, Raoul Hafner, chief designer (helicopters), Mrs V. Bonner, Dr A.E. Russell, chief designer, and Charles K. Bonner, design administration engineer.

4X-AGC, the third of El Al-Israel Airways' four Britannia 313s parked in front of the terminal building at Lod Airport.

Britannia G-ANCD, in temporary Cubana de Aviacion markings, flew a 27,000 mile sales trip through Portugal, Spain, Cuba and Latin America in twenty-three days.

This long-range Britannia made a 5,100 miles 14hr 49min non-stop London–Vancouver polar flight on 29 June 1957. After a short sojourn in a Spanish field while owned by Ghana Airways, it flew with two British airlines until 1970.

This remarkable photograph was taken in 1960 to mark fifty years service as a director by Sir Stanley White. With him are members of the original company who had records of continuous service. It totalled 1,550 years! Back row, from the left: R. Warren, F. Bigg, G. Symon, A. Symon, E. Withers, S. Jones, A. Dukelow, W. Mee. Third row: G. Allen, W. Trott, W. Sparkes, G. Rubery, K. Hayward, Miss E. Garland, R. Powell, W. Godwin, R. Westcott. Second row: E. Bennett, V. Viner, F. Biggs, W. Cusdin, J. Joslin, E. Clark, R. Hearder, F. Ireland, H. Stiddard, F. Hemmings, P. Simister. Front row: R. Smith, W. Slatter, A. Bradford, C. Uwins, Sir Stanley White, W. Morgan, H. Jones, L. Whistler.

Bristol advertising promoted the Britannia as all 'space, pace and grace'. This view of Canadian Pacific's Short and Harland-built Britannia CF-CZC certainly shows off these attributes.

The fearsome-looking Type 188 was part of Concorde's research programme. Built of stainless steel, its job was to gather data on structural heating in prolonged supersonic flight.

The Type 188 prepares to get airborne. As cameramen are present, this could be the first flight, which took place on 14 April 1962. The two Type 188s were the only wholly Bristol-designed and built jet aircraft.

BRISTOL AC NEG. 76156

The first Type 188 tucks up its Dowty undercarriage and gets airborne, urged upwards by 12 tons of thrust from its Bristol Siddeley Gyron Junior engines.

As a Type 188 waits to fly at Filton, on finals is the Vulcan flying test bed for Concorde's Bristol Siddeley Olympus 593 turbo-fan engines. One can be seen below the Vulcan's fuselage.

*BRISTOL A/C NEG 77411*

New manufacturing techniques were required to build the stainless steel Type 188. Puddle-welding (i.e. controlled local fusion of the material to be joined beneath the arc struck from the electrode surrounded by an inert Argon atmosphere – phew!) solved many problems.

*BRISTOL A/C NEG 76729*

The sleek, shiny Type 188 pops a braking parachute to shorten its landing run.

The Type 221D was the Fairey FD.2 modified at Filton. The fuselage was lengthened and a Concorde-style ogee-shaped wing was embodied to obtain data on its flight characteristics.

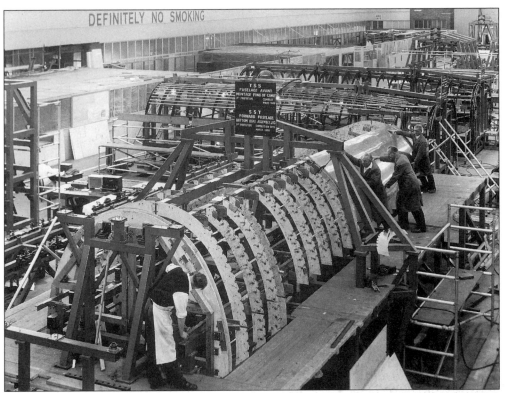

The front fuselage of the first British Concorde being built at Filton. The English-French signboards show March 1966 as completion date for this 'bottom boat assembly'.

Cockpit mock-up for Concorde demonstrating the drooping nose and retractable visor which was raised to reduce drag in supersonic cruise. Hydraulic jacks lifted the mock-up to simulate Concorde's nose-high landing attitude.

The first British Concorde nears completion in the Brabazon hangar at Filton, while the second one is being assembled alongside.

Overhaul of USAF F-111 swing-wing attack aircraft (foreground), and conversion of ex-airline BAC VC-10s to RAF tanker aircraft, for in-flight refuelling, photographed at Filton on 9 May 1984.

The signboard on this articulated vehicle reads 'Convoi Exceptionnel'. Being loaded in the early 1990s are Filton-built A320 Airbus wing sections destined for Airbus Industrie's Toulouse plant.

# Acknowledgements

Compiling a book such as this, which is intended to record, inform and entertain, cannot be a solo effort, for without photographs it would be dull indeed. I am, therefore, indebted to many people who opened their albums and archives, produced a host of exciting unpublished pictures and kindly loaned them to me. Chief among them are David Charlton, chief photographer of British Aerospace, Filton, and George Lambe, the Company archivist; Mike Hooks, renowned aviation author and photographer; John Oliver, Press Officer, Rolls-Royce, Bristol; and Malcolm Hall.

I am grateful to Mike Sivier at the *Bristol Journal*, who enabled me to contact many other people who have lent me photographs and provided historical detail. They are Charles Bonner, Andrew Boulton, Mrs Sidonie Frise, whose late husband, Leslie, was chief engineer and designer of the company, Reginald Gray, Mrs Mavis Grimshaw, Gordon Hewlett, Norman Kell, who sent photographs from his home in Spain, Mrs F.L. King, Leslie Mealing, Jack Pizey, cousin of 1911 company pilot Collyns Pizey, Miss Mavis Rogers, Mrs Elizabth Thomas, neice of Sir Roy Fedden, Mrs Margaret Uppington, whose parents first met on top of a tram travelling to work at Filton, and Sir George White, great-grandson of the company's founder. They helped to make this book a real Bristol family album. I am grateful to many others who also kindly sent me photographs which, sadly, lack of space prevented me from using.

I am indebted to Alan Sutton of the Chalford Publishing Company for his help during the creation of this book. My special thanks go, yet again, to my wife for editing my words on our PC and turning them into readable English on a small flat disk.

Derek N. James IEng, AMRAeS
Barnwood, Gloucester
October 1995